* THE MARSHES
Lighthouse

THE Point

CHESAPEAKE
BAY

WORMLEY CREEK

CESTER
oint

Point of
Rocks

WATERVIEW
FARM

Goodwin
Neck

CRAB
Neck

CHISMAN
CREEK

Temple
Farm

Ship Point

Fish
Neck

Poquoson

ROUTE 17

ty

Cockle
Town

Newport News

Hampton

# YORKTOWN,

## As I Remember

# YORKTOWN,

## As I Remember

By

Lucy  Hudgins  O'Hara

Edited  By

Katie  O'Hara  James

McClure Printing Company, Inc.

Printed by McClure Printing Company, Inc.
Verona, Virginia, U. S. A.

# DEDICATION

To Letty
For Her Inspiration

# PREFACE

The memories contained within this little book were originally intended for my children and grandchildren. With so many changes occurring so rapidly in the Twentieth Century, I began to realize that they didn't know the Yorktown that I knew at all! And that, I felt, was a shame.

It seemed to me that the early years of my life were an interesting time to be alive, and I thought that it would be interesting to my family to know how we lived here in Yorktown in those days also.

My inspiration for putting the memories down on paper came from a good friend, Letty Sheild Scott, who also grew up in Yorktown, just a few years after I did.

Some time ago, Letty came by to visit one day, and as we sat chatting I began to reminisce about her mother and other people I had known in the old days. She was quite impressed with some of the little stories I told her, and said she had never heard them before! It was at that point that she told me she thought I should write them down.

I remember she said, "Lucy, why don't you write down all of these things that you know about? You go on and write them down," she repeated, "while you can do it."

Because of her encouragement I did begin to write them down, little by little. And so, it's to Letty Sheild Scott that I dedicate these anecdotes. Without her inspiration, they would still exist only in my mind, and the memories of a few of my contemporaries who remain with us today.

I should state, at this point, that this little book is in no way a genealogy. No attempt has been made to describe, or even list all of my relatives.

Also, I would be the first to acknowledge that there were many wonderful people — both friends and neighbors — living in Yorktown during these years that I have not mentioned. My intent, as I said earlier, was simply to put down on paper some of my early memories of life in this little town. If particular people happened to be a part of those memories, they were included. I hope the rest will not take offense. None was intended.

Lucy Hudgins O'Hara
Yorktown, Virginia
March 7, 1981

# TABLE OF CONTENTS

# ILLUSTRATIONS

# YORKTOWN,

## As I Remember

Lucy Virginia Hudgins on the porch of her Ballard Street home in Yorktown, Va. about 1911.

My mother, Malvina Powell Hudgins, who was born at Shadow in Mathews County, Va. in 1857. She died in Yorktown on Dec. 26, 1927.

# CHAPTER I

# MY FAMILY

Yorktown to me is a very special little town, and my early memories of it are of beauty and fun. I can shut my eyes and see the shuffling, dancing feet of a youngster passing by my home at break of day, singing merrily along and telling the world how happy he is — "Just because she made those goo-goo eyes!"[1]

If I listen very closely, I can hear the pounding of horses hoofs, the blasting horn of a ship gliding by on the York River, or the lovely sound of a banjo serenade at twilight.

I can even smell the fragrance of honeysuckle, and feel my eyes almost blinded by the brilliance of scotchbroom blooming in abundance along the hillsides — each bush literally bursting with its thousands of bright yellow blossoms.

Flowers of one sort or another were everywhere in Yorktown during spring and summer. I remember one Easter morning in particular. The family was preparing for breakfast, and the sun was shining brightly across the table in a very festive way, but we did not have any flowers gracing it for the occasion. Suddenly, my sister Bertha left the room. In a short while she returned with her arms full of fruit blossoms she had gathered from somewhere nearby. How lovely they looked to me as the family gathered around the table on that glorious Easter morning.

Our first home in Yorktown was the Mallicote House (now called the Edmund Smith House) on Nelson Street. It was originally built around 1750.[2] When we moved in, almost 150 years later, the house had a front porch built high up from the ground with a rail around it. Once, when I was a small child, I was climbing around on the outside of the rail when I suddenly fell and broke my leg.

As I recall, the basement area of the house was used for the kitchen and dining room. Near the back entrance there were two rows of boxwood bushes that had grown into trees with benches built under them — and that's where I would play with my dolls.

My family moved into the Mallicote House when I was three months old. I was actually born in Fish Neck (which is now called Dare) out in York County. Up to that time my father had been a schoolteacher both in Cockle Town (now known as Grafton) and in

Poquoson. But, a short while after my birth on June 3, 1893, Papa (Theophilus Trimyer Hudgins) was elected to the office of York County Clerk of the Court, and he and Mama (Malvina Powell Hudgins) moved us all into town. (He continued, incidentally, to serve as Clerk of the Court until 1917 when he passed away at the age of 67.)

Papa had been born out in the county too, at Ship Point — an old farm that had been in the family for many years. When he lived there with three brothers and four sisters, it consisted of many acres of farm and woodland, and a three-story house on Chisman Creek.

Like many other people, my grandfather and grandmother (Thomas and Lucina Hudgins) owned slaves and made their living by farming and producing all that the family and servants needed right there on the farm at Ship Point.[3] Their way of life was probably fairly typical for that era.

My mother's people, too, had farmed, but they lived on the other side of the York River — at a place called Shadow over in Mathews County where she was born. My first cousin, Charles Powell, Sr., still lives there in the old home today.

My mother's parents (Lewis and Mary Powell) died while she was still fairly young, and for a while she moved to Baltimore to live with an older sister, Lucy, for whom I am named.[4] Later on, while still a young girl, my mother came to York County to visit a brother who was also a farmer — and it was then that she met my father.

Before the War Between the States, York County was really quite prosperous — with extensive farming. People raised all kinds of crops, including corn and tobacco. Vast acres of timber were also grown, cut by handsaws, and then drawn by horses to sawmills for processing into lumber. Local seafood, too, provided a living for many — and Wormley Creek oysters were noted and served in famous hotels in New York and other cities.

Some of this, of course, is still going on today, but more of it was going on when I was a little girl. I remember my mother, for instance, asking me to sit out on the front porch to watch for the fish sellers as they came up the hill from the river about ten o'clock in the morning. They used hooks and lines to catch their fish, and brought them to our door fresh (still alive usually), and selling for ten cents a bunch!

I also remember hearing minstrels imitate the farmhands who used to live out in the county during those early days. As they

My father, Theophilus Trimyer Hudgins, who served as York County Clerk of the Court from 1893 until his death on March 15, 1917. He was born at Ship Point in Fish Neck on Nov. 18, 1850.

Photo courtesy of Mrs. Milton Murray

My grandfather, Thomas Diggs Hudgins, who lived at Ship Point, York County, Va. during the War Between the States and until his death on Aug. 28, 1885. He was born on Dec. 13, 1812.

traveled down the road with their big loads of tobacco on their way to the markets in Richmond, it seems they would sing a little song that went like this: "Going down to Richmond town, to take my 'backie downtown."

At the beginning of the War Between the States my father's early home, Ship Point, was occupied as a Confederate camp. As the northern troops penetrated further and further south, however, the Confederates had to evacuate. Finally, Ship Point was taken over by a Union regiment. My Aunt Genie (Sarah Eugenia Hudgins) told us it was then used as the headquarters for two generals named Howard and Zuleski. My father was a small boy at that time — about 11 years old — but he and his entire family were forced to live under the enemy's control, and to use their own provisions to provide meals and comfort for the troops.

During this tragic time the family had to sacrifice everything of means, and of course its familiar way of life and happiness was broken up. My grandfather, Thomas Hudgins, was taken away as a prisoner by northern captors who were in hopes of drawing out information from him about the Confederate troops. My grandmother, Lucina Hudgins, was ill at the time, however, so the officer in charge gave orders not to disturb "the old lady." He seemed to be very considerate of her according to my father.

Papa meanwhile kept himself busy (as any mischievous boy might have done) by throwing sticks up at the attic window where a small room was used as a telegraph office for sending messages. As soon as the source of the racket was discovered, an officer would come to the window and shout, "Get away from there, you little rebel!"

When my aunts came to visit us, they would sit with my father and talk over all the tragedy and suffering they had had to endure: their father taken as a prisoner, losing a brother (Humphrey Hudgins) in the war, and the hardships that followed. They told us that after the war ended the South was in a state of poverty. Food was scarce, rationing was in effect, and people had to drive a long distance into Yorktown to get their allotment. Since slavery had been abolished, they explained to us, there were no "hands" to till the soil, or plant corn and tobacco as before.

During all of this time of trouble, my father and his brothers and sisters were greatly impressed by the life of their mother, Lucina, who lived to be 83 years old. They were also impressed with the way she died, and wrote down some thoughts about that experience, as well as some early memories of her.

This is what they recorded: "At her home in York County, Va., upon the morning of Dec. 16, 1897, our dear mother, Mrs. Lucina F. Hudgins, after protracted illness, in the eighty-third year of her age, sweetly fell asleep in Jesus.

"In early life she became a Christian and united with the M.E. Church South. To the church of her choice, she proved her devotion, by doing all in her power to help and support its institutions.

"Her home was the preachers' home and nothing gave her more pleasure than to have them partake of her hospitality, and to give her means, time and attention towards making them comfortable.

"Though she lived to a ripe old age, she had for many years been a sufferer from an incurable disease; her sufferings at times were intense, but she bore them with Christian fortitude and resignation.

"In all the relations of life our dear mother was true and faithful. As a wife and mother she was devoted, kind and self-sacrificing; as a friend and neighbor, always ready and willing with kind words and deeds to add to their comfort.

"During her long life, she had many firery (sic) trials to pass through, but she found 'God's grace sufficient' in time of need.

"For weeks before the end came, she suffered intensely, but was calm and rational; rejoicing in the prospect of soon going to a home of eternal rest.

"God, in His providence, permitted her seven children to be constantly by her bedside. To each one of them she gave parting words of exhortation, commendation, blessing and farewell; beseeching them to meet her in heaven.

"God grant we may keep the promise made our dying mother; and follow in the footsteps of one, whose examples in everything that make a noble and exalted character, and an humble Christian, are worthy of imitation.

"When she came down to the dark river, God sent a cohort of angels and dear departed friends, to guide her over to the other side. She recognized them. Her husband (our father) who had preceded her to the better land twelve years ago, was the first to be recognized. Oh! How glad she was to go, and what an expression of ecstasy and delight, when she knew she was almost at her journey's end. We felt that around our mother's deathbed was a sacred place, though to our eyes, these heavenly visions were invisible.

"Her funeral services were conducted by Rev. J. F. White, assisted by her pastor Rev. J. S. Wallace. Many relatives and friends attended, anxious to pay this last tribute of respect to the dear depart-

Photo courtesy of Mrs. Louis Noah.

My grandmother, Lucina Foster Hudgins, who lived at Ship Point, York County, Va. during the War Between the States and until her death on Dec. 16, 1897. She was born on Oct. 17, 1815.

This photo, taken about 1945, is courtesy of Mr. and Mrs. Angelo Taylor Jennings. An aerial photo of my family home, Ship Point (just to the right of center), in Fish Neck (now called Dare), York County, Va.

ed, and to extend sympathy to the bereaved. Her three sons, one son-in-law, and two grandsons were pallbearers.

"We laid her to rest in Providence Churchyard by the side of our dear father, to whom for about fifty years she was a devoted helpmeet. 'There sweet be thy rest, til He bid thee arise, To hail Him in triumph, descending the skies.' " The account is simply signed, "Her Children."[5]

While my father and his sisters talked about the past, we children would sit on our "crickets" (what you would now call little stools) listening with wide open eyes to all the sad happenings and sorrow they had experienced at Ship Point. Everything they said made a great impression on me, and gave me a bitter and resentful feeling toward those terrible Yankees. (I didn't know then, of course, that I would end up loving and marrying one!)

Miss Mary Eliza was one aunt who visited us quite often when I was young. She was a spinster, and the eldest of my father's brothers and sisters. I remember her as being very proper and dignified. Her hair was an auburn shade, and she wore it parted down the middle of her head with a little knot at the back.

When she came to visit, Aunt Mary Eliza would spend hours rocking back and forth in a chair, her knitting needles clicking. Most often she knitted socks, but sometimes she sewed little strips of calico in various colors together in different designs to be made into a quilt. It always seemed impossible to me, though, that those little pieces of calico would one day become a big quilt!

My father's sister, Kitty, and her husband, Uncle Joe Hogge, lived out at Waterview Farm, which they managed at that time for a family that lived in New York, and sometimes we would drive out to visit them. Waterview, back in those days, was one big farm extending all the way from the York River out to Goodwin Neck Road. As I recall, it was a great place for hunting and horseback riding. We children particularly liked to visit Aunt Kitty and Uncle Joe, however, because they raised peacocks, and as we drove up the birds would spread out their beautiful tail feathers for us to see. (Most everyone at that time had a bunch of peacock feathers arranged in a tall vase, and placed in their parlor on the piano, or on a table.)

When my aunt and uncle lived at Waterview, a long lane led up to the big house with a peach orchard on either side. As you approached the house there were two gates to be opened — one at the entrance to the lane, and another up near the house. I'll never forget those two gates, because unfortunately it always seemed to be my job to get out and open them when we drove up for a visit!

# CHAPTER II

## LIFE ON BALLARD STREET

When we left the Mallicote House and moved to Ballard Street, around 1898, my family lived in a large frame house with eight bedrooms. And, because we had more room than we needed, from time to time we took in boarders, whom we called "guests." I remember a sign swinging from our front porch brightly proclaimed "River View — Private Entertainment." That attracted our "guests" — who consisted of transients, "drummers" (now known as traveling salesmen), schoolteachers who taught in the community, and others just visiting Yorktown for its beach and view, or historic points of interest.

One afternoon we were all sitting out on the front porch when a little girl named Catherine (who later grew up and married the man who became Admiral John J. Ballentine) walked past on her way to visit her grandmother (Frances Howard Sheild), who lived at the bottom of the hill. Catherine was only about five years old at the time, but she was very bright — precocious really — and apparently already well-versed in the history of Yorktown.

When she saw us, Catherine stopped to talk as she often did. But, on this particular day she paused suddenly in mid-sentence, and ran over and peered down into a rainbarrel that we had outside to catch water for flowers. Just as suddenly she popped up again and loudly exclaimed, "Oh, Mrs. Hudgins, come see what's here!" Before my startled mother could get there to find out though, Catherine suddenly pealed out again, "It's Cornwallis hiding in your rainbarrel!"

Cornwallis, the general who had headed up the British forces in Yorktown during the Revolutionary War, was still well-known for his "cave" down on the waterfront. Some people said he planned to hide there from Washington, and others said the cave connected to a tunnel with an entrance in the Nelson House, where he then lived. The idea was that he would escape, if necessary, through the tunnel and hop on a waiting ship down on the river. Neither plan worked, and of course he had been dead for many, many years. Because of Catherine though, I always think of him as just hiding — in my mother's rainbarrel![1]

As was customary in those days, Mama served our dinner around noon, and supper at six. Evening was considered to be from one o'clock 'til dark — then it was night. But, after the Yankees came with their northern habits, we never knew if evening was night, or if it was afternoon — or if supper was dinner, or just when and where lunch ever did come in!

We all had our own gardens, and raised fowl and cured meat for home use, and had a cow to provide milk as well. Hog-killing day was gruesome for me. Before dawn men would arrive with a big iron pot for scalding the pigs after they were killed. I would run and hide to avoid hearing the squealing.

After the pigs were slaughtered, the hams were smoked over hickory chips and bark in a little building out behind our house called a "smokehouse." We had to keep the fire smouldering all during the day, and often smoke would seep through the cracks in the walls. On one occasion a visitor riding through town stopped and came to our door and told us a house outside was on fire. We thanked him and told him not to worry, as it was just the hickory smoke curing the hams!

Another outdoor job occurred when we had to wash the family clothes and linens. During fair weather the wooden tubs and washboard would be brought outside and placed under a shade tree. Hot water then had to be brought from the kitchen. Even though it was a toilsome job, the aroma of Mama's homemade soap drifting through the air, and the sound of the snow-white sheets swishing in the breeze, made laundry day a very gratifying experience.

During most of the year, of course, we children went to school. My brothers and sisters and I were taught in a one-room schoolhouse on Main Street that was located where the Hornsby House is now, right next to my present home across from the Victory Monument.

The first teacher I remember was Miss Katie Stryker, a lovely lady who later married Mr. Conway Howard Sheild and had the precocious daughter, Catherine. The year she first taught me I was not actually of school age. As I was the youngest child in my family, however, and didn't want to stay home without the others, Miss Katie allowed me to attend school with my brother, Tom, and sister, Lillie, as long as I would behave and not disturb the other pupils.[2] Being the youngest, I was allowed to lead the procession as we marched in and out of the schoolroom. How proud I was!

In Miss Katie's school we often had spelling matches, and we had calisthenics during both morning and afternoon sessions. We also had a ten-minute recess. But, for me, the best part of the day was geography class.

In one corner of the room stood a square, shallow box on a tall stand. The box was filled with clean white sand brought up from the beach. It was used for the geography class. With a pitcher of water at hand, we were allowed to form rivers, islands, mountains and the like, and this was how I spent most of my time that first year. In retrospect, the practice did help me to remember the geography Miss Katie taught, and so was actually of benefit to me in later years when I was truly a member of the class.

I'll never forget how sweet and patient Miss Katie was — but she believed in discipline too! If any of us misbehaved, we were punished by having to stand in a corner of the room facing the wall. There was always much giggling by the other pupils, which added — of course — to our embarrassment and punishment.

Another schoolteacher whom I loved and will never forget was Miss Annie West, who boarded in our home and took her meals with us. Miss Annie was a spinster, very well educated, and a good Christian woman. She dressed very nicely, and I particularly remember sitting in her lap and playing with some black beads she used to wear around her neck.

In addition to teaching me second and third grade, Miss Annie was like a member of the family, and when she became ill and passed away, we were all very sad. Her family came for the funeral service, which was held in our parlor. I remember my cousin, Cossie Powell (who later became Mrs. John E. Wornam), sang "Asleep in Jesus," and then Miss Annie was taken back to her home in Manchester (now called South Richmond) for interment.

During most of these years, my sister Mary was not in Yorktown with us. Interestingly, when I was very small she went back to live in Mathews, just a few miles from where my mother had been born. Here she made her home with my father's sister, Aunt Genie, and her husband, Charles Hudgins (a cousin), who had no children. Later she married Mr. Ellis C. Richardson, also of Mathews.

Lucy (left), Tom (center) and Lillie (right) Hudgins about the time they were being taught by Miss Katie Stryker in a little one-room schoolhouse on Main Street, in Yorktown, Va. Photo approximately 1898. Lillie later became Mrs. Charles A. Walthall.

A 1911 photo of the Nelson House, built by "Scotch Tom" in the early 1700s. I loved the old house at Christmas. What fun it was each year with gifts, candy and other delicious sweets the Cruikshanks would pass out to all the children in the neighborhood.

# CHAPTER III

# OUR NEIGHBORS

The Nelson House, built by "Scotch Tom" in the early 1700s, has always been a major attraction in Yorktown.[1] When I was a little girl it had an entrance on Main Street consisting of brick steps leading up to a walk that went to the front door. On either side of the brick steps was a wide seat made of a stone slab. Boxwood bushes formed a screen around the front. We children enjoyed running up and down those front steps as we walked back and forth to school, as well as sitting on the cool seats on a warm summer day.

From either spot near the front entrance, we could see a tree said to have actually been planted by Lafayette while he was visiting at the Nelson House during his return visit to the United States in 1824.[2] The tree appears in a picture I still have that was taken about 1915. Unfortunately, it died during the 1930s.

During the time my family lived in the Mallicote House, the Nelson House was occupied by a family by the name of Cruikshank, who had previously lived at Temple Farm (now known as the Moore House). The Cruikshanks were originally from Pennsylvania. But, even though some resentment and bitterness still existed towards Northerners when they moved here, this family — being very kind and friendly — soon gained its way into the hearts of the old residents of Yorktown.

The Cruikshanks had a large family of girls and boys (as we also had), and being close neighbors I loved to run in to see them. What a thrill it was to see the spacious rooms with high ceilings; the tall, wide formal staircase in the entrance hall; and even the dark, narrow, winding upper stairs that led all the way to the attic.

The young people in Yorktown would gather at the Nelson House for parties, and to sing around the big grand piano. At Christmas the house would be decorated with garlands of evergreens and holly. A large tree was always placed in the library, and covered with sparkling tinsel, strung popcorn and bright ornaments. Surrounding the tree was a miniature village with houses, trees, animals, and a baby in a manger — all depicting the birth of Christ.

What fun it was each year with gifts, candy and other delicious sweets the Cruikshanks would pass out to all the children in the neighborhood. Though we had our own Christmas tree and stockings hung on the mantle, this big house with its festive appearance provided many happy occasions that I still remember fondly.

One of our other neighbors on Nelson Street was an elderly lady of German descent who spoke only broken English. Mrs. Beer was very kind and neighborly, and made delicious gingerbread that she shared with her friends. When we children saw her coming we would all exclaim, " 'Ach' to goodness, here comes the gingerbread lady!" " 'Ach' to goodness" was one of her favorite expressions.[3]

A very nice family by the name of Stryker also lived in town, just about where the Duke of York Motel is now located. They were of Dutch descent. As I recall, the husband spoke very rapidly, and not very plainly, and one time he came to our door all excited, saying what sounded like "series, series tonight!" My mother became somewhat alarmed, thinking he was trying to say "serious, serious," and that someone in the family was ill. After much questioning, however, she finally understood. It seems that their "night-blooming cereus" — a very rare and fragrant plant which only blooms at long intervals and only at midnight — would be blooming that night, and Mr. Stryker was inviting us to come and see it!

This same couple, Henry and Caroline Stryker, were the parents of the "Miss Katie" of my early school years. Sometime later, they also became the proud grandparents of both the precocious Catherine and another darling little girl who carried a basketful of golden Yorktown buttercups in my wedding procession. She and my niece, Elizabeth Wainwright, served as "flower girls" in the cermony, and scattered the buttercups down the aisle to decorate my path to the altar. We townspeople all know this little girl today as Letty Sheild Scott.[4]

Another lady named Baxter lived in a small house to the west of us on Nelson Street that is no longer standing. To make a little money, she sold notions. Everyone in town at that time did their own sewing, or had their clothes made by a dressmaker who stayed in the home until everything was finished. Therefore, these items were in great demand. We bought them too, of course, for our family sewing — a lot of which was done by my mother and my eldest sister Bertha when I was small.

Because of this, I remember being very put out with my sister Bertha's fiance, Mr. Jacob ("Jake") Wainwright. Once when he came to visit shortly before they were married, I told him, "You can't take my sister away, because then I won't have anyone to make my clothes!" Much to my chagrin, he did take her away though — all

A 1915 photograph of the tree (left) in front of the Nelson House said to have been planted by Lafayette during his return visit to the United States in 1824. It died during the 1930s. (The three children were visitors in town.)

An early photo of the Thomas Sessions House, built between 1692 and 1699. When I was a young girl, a widow named Minson lived there. Her daughter, Alice, was married in the parlor to our family doctor, Stafford Cooke.

the way to Fish Neck! Later, they did move back into town, and for many years — until her death at the age of 101 in 1978 — my sister Bertha lived in a brick house not too far from the Mallicote House on Nelson Street.

When I was small, Mrs. Minson, who was a widow, lived directly across the street from the Nelson House. She and her daughters lived in what is now called the Thomas Sessions House. It is said to be the oldest in Yorktown.[5] While they lived there one of Mrs. Minson's daughters, Alice, was married to our family physician, Dr. Stafford Cooke. The ceremony was held in the parlor. After Mrs. Minson died, Mr. Sheild bought the house, and it was here that Catherine and Letty grew up.

During those early years there were no buildings on Main Street, or Monument Road (recently renamed Zweybrucken Street for the Duke of Zweybrucken and his troops from the German town of the same name who successfully led the attack on Redoubt 9 during the Revolutionary War) beyond the Victory Monument itself. There was an old road running off from Monument Road to the southeast through the fortifications, that according to local tradition was called the Fort Gate. When I was small, the gate itself was still there.

I also remember a road leading down to Cornwallis' Cave through The Great Valley, which is located just across Main Street from the Nelson House. One frequent user of that road was a man who drove an ox cart down to fill a barrel with water from the well at the foot of the cliff. The family that lived there in the Fisherman's Cottage (which is now known as the Archer Cottage) held the key that opened the big wooden door to the cave for visitors. They charged ten cents admission, but children were admitted free.

Visiting our neighbors after dark on any of the streets of Yorktown in those days could be quite hazardous. You see, the county then had a law known as the "No-Fence Law," and consequently cattle sometimes roamed freely. Since we had no street lights, and often only a dim light shining from someone's window to guide our way, we had to be careful, from time to time, to avoid stumbling over a cow sleeping peacefully in the middle of the road!

To make matters worse, neither Main Street nor any of the other streets in Yorktown were hard surfaced at that time. As a result, they alternated between being very muddy in bad weather and very sandy when dry. In addition, they always seemed to be in rough condition, due to the ox carts and horse-drawn wagons loaded with cord wood, or barrels of water being delivered to the people in town who didn't have their own supply.

The everyday travel of ordinary people didn't help the condition of the roads either. For family use two-wheel jumpers and four-wheel buggies were in evidence everywhere. Along with a few others, however, we had a carriage with fringe around the top. When it rained, there were curtains that had to be buttoned to the carriage on the outside. The one in front had isinglass windows to see through while driving.

The horse that pulled our carriage was named "Betty." She was very tame and gentle, but gave birth to a colt we raised that was just the opposite — quite wild and spirited! "Uncle" William, a colored man who worked for us, understood the nature of horses, though, and eventually broke him in to be a good horse for the family. I remember we named him "York."

# CHAPTER IV

# OTHER CHARACTERS

Another old Yorktown house that I recall stood on the corner of Main and Read Streets. It was built of brick and was occupied by colored people.[1] On one side of the house lived "Aunt" Rachel Walker, a very stout, neat person who walked with a cane and wore a starched white apron and dust cap.[2] She would appear on the street on sunny days — particularly when court was in session — with a basket of fresh-roasted peanuts selling for five cents a bag. They cost ten times that today and don't taste nearly as good!

Like many other people in those days, "Aunt" Rachel had some right amusing expressions that you don't hear too much any more. When we would meet her on the street and say, "Good morning, 'Aunt' Rachel, how you feeling?" she would often reply, "I ain't so many this morning." We never knew quite where she got those words, but assumed they meant she wasn't feeling too well! At other times we would ask her, "Where you going this morning, 'Aunt' Rachel?" and she would reply, "I done been where I'se guine!"

In a portion of "Aunt" Rachel's house lived "Aunt" Cilla and "Uncle" Bob Harrod. "Aunt" Cilla cooked and did housework for people in town, and "Uncle" Bob cut stove wood. They had a daughter named Clara-Bob, who was the lazy type. She could most often be seen sitting on the front doorsill with her baby in her arms — a typical old country-town scene. The house they lived in burned about the year 1911.

Near "Aunt" Cilla and "Uncle" Bob's, across Read Street, was a building then called the Cooper House, and now known as the Thomas Pate House.[3] It was occupied by a Mrs. Cooper, who also had a notion store in a front room of the building where she sold spool cotton, pins, needles, and the like.

A Mrs. Goodall, who was a very old woman, shared part of this house. She was of English descent, and proudly spoke of her son who she said was an Anglican minister living in England. Other than that, Mrs. Goodall was a rather mysterious person, though, and told very little of her own past life. I remember her as a very untidy person who always wore long black drabby dresses. This, plus the queer accent, gave her a slightly "witchy-looking" appearance, and she terrified us children!

Mrs. Goodall sold eggs and chickens, and being very poor she would comb the beach for driftwood that she could bring up and burn in her stove. People were very good to her, as I recall, and gave her food and clothing. She would often come to our house on Saturday carrying a basket for my mother to drop food in. After receiving it, she would show her appreciation by saying, "God bless you." Sometimes on a cold winter day we would take her hot soup, and she would struggle to the door, her face smutty from burning the wet, soggy wood. When Mrs. Goodall finally passed away, she was buried by the county, with the help of town citizens.

Another of old Yorktown's many interesting characters was a very prominent citizen, whom I always thought of as being quite aristocratic. He was also very active and energetic, and had a habit of walking up and down the street several times during the day. Along the way, he would stop in each of the stores and pick up a gingersnap here and a few peanuts there to munch on while walking down to the beach. The whole time, of course, this gentleman by the name of Mr. Conway Howard Sheild (Miss Katie's husband, and Catherine and Letty's father) was speaking and running on with everyone he met.

It was well-known around town that if anyone wished to see Mr. Sheild for business, or any other reason, they could be told to just stand anywhere on the street and wait, and very soon they would see him pass by!

In the early 1900s Mr. Sheild served as Commonwealth Attorney for York County for a number of years, but I remember him best as a tall, sprightly person who was very fond of children. He always seemed to notice them. Once, after I was married, my small son, Leslie, was sitting on our porch step as Mr. Sheild walked by eating peanuts. He stopped to speak to little Les and handed him a few. Hoping for some manners from my son, I then looked at him and asked, "Now, what should you say?" To my horror he immediately replied, "Give me another one!" [4]

About this same time, a charming old couple with the famous name of "Roosevelt" lived just outside of town on property that became part of the Navy Mine Depot (now known as the Naval Weapons Station). They were originally from Chicago, and were actually distant relatives of President Franklin Roosevelt. Everyone loved them, and they were affectionately called "Granny" and "Daddy" Roosevelt.

Mrs. Roosevelt, as I recall, was very pretty — tall and erect. Her snow white hair added much to her dignity, and her keen sense of humor much to her personality. She told many amusing stories,

This photo, courtesy of Letty Sheild Scott, was taken in 1912.

Mr. Conway Howard Sheild, who served as Commonwealth Attorney for York County during the early 1900s.

This 1918 photo is courtesy of Letty Sheild Scott.

Mrs. Conway Howard Sheild, my first schoolteacher and the organizing directress for the Yorktown Branch of the Association for the Preservation of Virginia Antiquities.

including one on her husband. Immediately after their wedding, as they were about to leave by train for their honeymoon, he apparently stepped aside to pick up a newspaper while she went on and boarded. The train then pulled out, leaving Mr. Roosevelt stranded on the platform of the depot with the tickets in his coat pocket!

Poor Mrs. Roosevelt then had to explain it all to the conductor, which she always told us she did with much emotional trembling and embarrassment! The happy couple was finally reunited — but not until the following day.

When the government took over most of the Navy Mine Depot area during World War I, many families had to vacate their homes, but this dear old couple was allowed to remain. Unfortunately, a short while afterwards their home burned. Then the Roosevelts built a small house on Nelson Street where they lived until they eventually passed away. This house is still standing today across from the Captain John Ballard House.

# CHAPTER V

## "COLORED" CUSTOMS[1]

During Reconstruction days, after the War Between the States ended, some of the colored people who had lived in York County went north to find jobs, but others remained. At the same time, some who had been in the north came south to live. One of these, a Mr. Robert McNorton, became a member of the state legislature from this district. Later, another colored man, Mr. James Mitchell, held the job of Deputy Collector of Customs in charge of the Port of Yorktown.

When I was a young girl, a big celebration was held in Yorktown on May 30th by all of the colored people from near and far. Each year on this day, called "Emancipation Day," they celebrated the ending of the institution of slavery in the United States, and some walked a long distance to participate.

To begin the celebration, a tall stately man riding horseback would lead a parade up Yorktown hill along Ballard Street. He was followed by other men, women and children — keeping step to the music of a local band and carrying picnic baskets. They were always dressed up in their Sunday-best clothes, and I often remember thinking I never had seen so much red, yellow and pink ribbon on heads and hats in all my life!

As part of this colorful scene, one particular man would appear each year selling homemade ice cream and lemonade. To attract attention to his wares, he would call out in a loud voice: "Ice cold lemonade......made in the shade......sold in the sun......if you don't come quick......you won't get none!"

Everything was very orderly on "Emancipation Day," though, and the citizens of the town cheerfully gave way to the marchers and spectators, knowing it to be their day to celebrate and enjoy. After the parade and ceremonies were over on Main Street, the participants would go on to their own cemetery back of the U. S. National Cemetery.[2] There they would hold a memorial service and lay flowers on the graves.

When I was small, the colored people in Yorktown also had a custom of holding their baptism ceremonies every summer down on the beach. These ceremonies would follow revival meetings held in their church. As I recall, there would be many days of "seeking" and "meditating," and then suddenly the people would appear on the street shaking hands with everyone they met, and singing with great joy such words of repentance as: "Thank God Almighty, my soul is free from the very thoughts of sin!"

After the "seeking" and "meditating" were over, and repentance had been accomplished, the baptism ceremonies would be held. On the appointed Sunday the congregation would gather at the river's edge, and one of the deacons, wearing a long black robe and carrying a pole, would go out to test the depth and safety of the water. He was always followed by the minister, who would be wearing a white robe. The minister would lead those to be baptized, who were also dressed in long white robes and had white kerchiefs tied around their heads, out into the water.

Meanwhile, the rest of the congregation would be joyfully singing a hymn with great reverence. In the open air this singing was truly beautiful. I remember being particularly struck by how the voices all blended together in harmony. With other spectators, I would stand close by in order to be able to hear everything clearly and fully enjoy the event.

At times during the ceremony there would be great shouting and emotion, and the minister and deacons would be compelled to restrain those being baptized. On one occasion, over the noise of the crowd, someone claimed to hear a loud voice sing out, "I don't want you to hold me......I want 'Brother' Jones to hold me!" A little romance, it seems, was entering into the occasion!

# CHAPTER VI

## SHOPKEEPERS, PHYSICIANS, & POLITICIANS

Around the turn of the century, when I was growing up here, Yorktown did not have a fancy grocery store or butcher shop. But, there was a butcher who came to our door driving a horse and covered wagon. He sold beef and lamb, etc., cut just as you wished there on the spot! Hucksters also came by selling chickens and eggs, as well as fruit and vegetables they had just gathered — often with the dew still sparkling on them.

We did have several people who ran "general stores" in town. They sold groceries, drygoods, rubber coats and boots used by watermen, household goods and even some medicines — since there was no drugstore nearby. Workmen would often stop in at lunchtime to pick up cheese and crackers, and gingersnaps.

In these stores the candy case with its rolling top was the greatest attraction for us children. We seldom had more than a penny to spend, and consequently would stand on our tiptoes for quite a while to view the great assortment of mouth watering candy — trying to decide which was the largest piece, or just how many we could get for one penny!

Sometimes "Uncle" William would drive my mother and sister, Lillie, and me to Cockle Town (now known as Grafton) where we shopped for hats, dress goods, lace and other trimmings, etc. We bought them from Mrs. William Wainwright who had a shop set up in a portion of her husband's general store. It offered men's apparel and groceries, as well as most anything else one needed.

There was also a store for ladies' needs in Crab Neck (now called Seaford). This store, too, sold millinery making and all sorts of trimmings for hats. Most ladies' hats seemed to look the same in those days. Maybe they would have a different quill feather, or a different bow of ribbon, but they all had a very similar style — as one could plainly see at church on Sunday!

In addition to the "general stores," peddlers would often find their way to Yorktown carrying heavy packs on their backs filled with all kinds of linens and laces, etc. They would go from door to door showing their wares. In dealing with these peddlers, we soon learned that much bargaining had to go on before a fair price could be decided upon.

Mr. H. M. Clements' general store about 1918. When I was a small girl, this old building was used by Mr. Robert Chandler, Sr. for making carriages and buggies. Here it's decorated for Yorktown Day.

Photo courtesy of Edith M. Elliott.

This 1925 photo is courtesy of Theresa B. Gammage. When I was a young woman, the ladies of Yorktown would gather at The Spinning Wheel Shop on Main Street (third from left) to visit as well as to see the antiques. Many have been thrilled by owning one of them.

During the springtime an organ-grinder would appear also, with a monkey perched on his back. The monkey wore a red vest trimmed in gold buttons, and a red cap. He would immediately attract all the children in town, who then proceeded to trail along behind him. The organ-grinder would walk through town stopping in front of everyone's door, and the little monkey would dance and perform while the music went on and on — as long as the coins kept jingling into the cup!

I also remember gypsies roaming around the countryside from time to time. They would settle down somewhere near town pitching their tents and telling fortunes. When the news got around, everyone locked their barn doors and kept their children inside until the gypsies were well on their way!

There was a carriage shop on Main Street when I was small where carriages, buggies, and other vehicles were actually built by Mr. Robert Chandler, Sr. Later this building was taken over by Mr. H. M. Clements and run as a general store. There was also a black-smith shop on Ballard Street where people brought their horses to be shod. The blacksmith wore a canvas apron and toiled hard all day long. I can still hear the pounding of his heavy hammers and see the sparks fly from the red hot anvil as he shaped the shoe to each horse's hoof.

We didn't have an ice plant in Yorktown until I was a grown woman, and consequently while I was growing up ice was very scarce. It was shipped from West Point by boat in three hundred pound blocks — dripping all the way. The storekeepers and others who bought it in large quantities buried it in saw dust, but my family kept its small amount in an icebox. At times, I remember, ice would be so scarce it would be impossible to get a few pounds from a store for iced tea on a hot summer day.

We were fortunate though, because in earlier times, when my grandfather was alive, there weren't any ice plants at all. Like every-one else, his family had to chop ice from a frozen pond during the winter and then store it in the ground in what were known as "ice wells" for use throughout the rest of the year.

There were no drugstores in Yorktown when I was small either, and since the nearest one was in Williamsburg, we were often com-pelled to resort to home remedies. In the spring of the year, a mixture of sulphur and molasses was supposed to be a good tonic. We also took sage tea. For a headache and fever we used brown paper saturated in vinegar and placed on the forehead. We also had mustard plasters for chestcolds, and paregoric or essence of peppermint for stomach ache. Quinine and chill tonic were sold in abundance for malaria.

If the patient failed to respond to these remedies, a doctor was called. Like all other doctors at that time, our physician, Dr. Stafford Cooke, came to see us in our home when we were sick. Sometimes, he even had to leave his warm comfortable bed on a cold winter night to hitch up his horse and drive for miles to visit a sick person, or bring a baby into this world.

When the doctor arrived, the medicine case — filled with all sorts of pills of every conceivable color — was opened, and the right ones chosen for whatever ailment one had. The doctor then stayed until the patient responded to the treatment, visiting with the family. The bill for such a visit would be one or two dollars, but no charge was made for those unable to pay. The very conscientious ones, however, might reciprocate by giving food, vegetables, etc., that they had raised on their farms.

In addition to being our physician, Dr. Cooke and his family (I might add) were our friends. We used to visit back and forth, and I remember spending many a night out at the Cooke Farm on the old York-Hampton Road with his daughters Sally (who became Mrs. Thomas Sheild) and Mary (now Mrs. Douglas Hubbard of Newport News).

When I was growing up there weren't any antique shops in Yorktown either. It wasn't until about 1925 that the first one was opened on Main Street by a lovely, gracious southern lady who was also very dressy. On the first day of spring she would blossom out in a jonquil-yellow dress and a large yellow hat. This lady attended Grace Episcopal Church and often sat near me. I can still detect the fragrance of violets rising in the air as she pulled her dainty lace handkerchief out of her purse, and hear the jingling of her heavy charm bracelets.

Mrs. A. Y. Burcher was loved and admired by everyone. Ladies of the town would gather at her shop to visit and to see her antiques. Many have been thrilled by owning one of them — as well as by knowing this sweet little lady at The Spinning Wheel Shop.

The first postmaster I remember in Yorktown was a colored person by the name of Albert Christian. At that time the post office was set up in his own dwelling on Main Street where the Yorktown Pewter Shop was recently located. I remember a partition divided the waiting room from the area where mail was sorted. And, in one corner of the room was a small desk holding a bottle of ink and a pen.

Main Street in Yorktown about the year 1910. This old photograph shows the very familiar ox cart, which has just brought a barrel of water up through the Great Valley from the well at the bottom of the hill.

The County Clerk's Office used by my father and the adjacent fourth courthouse, which was built in 1875 on the site of the original at the corner of Main and Ballard Streets.

From an old postal card published by J. S. De Neufville.

Both in-coming and out-going mail were brought and carried by the same mailman, traveling by horse and buggy from Lee Hall. Since there was only one mail delivery during the day, everyone gathered for it — about eleven o'clock in the morning. Then, one by one, each person would appear before a little window as it was raised, to receive his or her letters and packages.

The postmaster also had a restaurant serving both white and colored people, but in different dining rooms. While in the post office, one could often detect the aroma of ham and cabbage drifting in from the kitchen. Albert Christian's wife, "Aunt" Sarah, being very thrifty, also made ice cream, turned and frozen by hand. It was served by the saucer on a fresh red-checkered tablecloth, or by the quart to be taken home.

At one time, I remember, there were two stores on Main Street in Yorktown side by side dealing in the same merchandise! One of them was operated by Mr. John De Neufville — whose daughter Marie (now Mrs. Edward Glaser of Williamsburg) was a schoolmate of mine. During the 1920s the post office was moved into one end of the second of these stores — which was run by Mrs. Harry H. Hamilton's grandfather, Mr. William Rodgers.

At another time the post office was located on the grounds of the Dudley Digges House, and then again it was in a small building on Church Street. No matter where it was located, though, it always seemed to be the custom to have the post office where people could also conveniently do their shopping.

Yorktown was founded in 1691, and six years later court was held in the first county courthouse on Lot 24 at the corner of Main and Ballard Streets. Four have been erected since then. The second courthouse, built about 1733, burned during the fire of 1814. The third, built in 1818, was destroyed during the year of 1863, when Union Army ammunition stored in it exploded. The York County Clerk's Office my father used was located right next to the fourth courthouse built in 1875. In 1940 this courthouse also burned and then court was held in the U.S.O. Building that stood where the courthouse parking lot is now located. The present courthouse was built in the same location as the first four in 1955.[1]

When my father was Clerk of the Court, there were only two rooms in the clerk's office. One was used as the office proper, and the other one (which was quite small) housed the old York County records dating back to the year 1633. During the time of the Civil War, these valuable records were saved by Mr. Boliver Sheild, who was then Clerk of the Court.[2] He had the foresight to see the danger of the records being destroyed by fire — and so, he loaded them in a boat and took them up the York River to the Mattaponi River and hid them in an ice house. They remained there safely until the war ended.

During my father's era, an old mulberry tree stood at the front of the courthouse with a bench built around it, where men would gather and sit to discuss politics and other topics of the day. There was also a well on the grounds where those who had no water on their own premises (mostly colored people) could bring buckets to fill. I have seen them with a bucket in each hand, as well as one balanced on their head — and all filled with water! I also remember a two story brick jail being near-by. We children would run hastily by it — afraid of seeing a prisoner at the barred windows. At that time food was carried to the men in baskets by the jailor, who had also prepared it.

When I was small, court was held on the first Monday of the month, but it sometimes was extended, owing to the importance and size of a particular docket. When court was in session, it was a very busy day for Yorktown. "Court Day," you see, was a time when busy farmers and merchants would take the day off in order to meet with people, and just generally enjoy the excitement. The courthouse yard would be filled with horses and buggies, and one would constantly hear the neighing of the horses, and occasionally some horse trading taking place too!

Because my mother had a sort of boarding house, on some occasions when there was a criminal case, the sheriff would bring the jurymen (who were often friends of my father) to our home for dinner.

I also remember one afternoon in particular when my father came home quite excited, and told us that he had just had the honor of showing the old York County records to the President of the United States, Mr. Woodrow Wilson! The President apparently was traveling incognito, and so had not made himself known, but my father recognized him. The President, he said, shook his hand and thanked him for his courtesy.

One of two old lighthouses that used to guide ships into the York River when I was a small girl. With no dust to contend with, I was always very envious of the tender's home! His family loved company — being so remote.

Lucy Hudgins (center) out for a stroll near the York River with Blanche (left) and Marshall (right) de Neufville about 1908.

# CHAPTER VII

# THE YORK RIVER

When I was a little girl Yorktown beach had snow white sand. It wasn't until later that marl was dug from the cliffs around the beach for surfacing the roads — which then began to wash down and discolor the beach. How peaceful and refreshing it was walking along the shoreline, and breathing in the salt water air and odor of fresh tar that would be circulating up and down the beach when Mr. Joseph (Joe) De Neufville was tarring his nets in preparation for the fishing season.

At that time Mr. De Neufville and his family lived in the Fisherman's Cottage (now known by its original name, the Archer Cottage) near Cornwallis' Cave.[1] I often walked down to his home to stroll along the beach and visit with his two daughters (now Mrs. Marshall Dadds and Mrs. Blanche Cobb), who were girlhood friends of mine.

In summer most everyone around went swimming ( or bathing as it was then called). The whole Yorktown community was like one big family going down on the beach about four o'clock. That was the best time because it was after the nap period. Also, with the sun lower in the sky there was less danger of getting sunburned. Even so, we all wore long bathing suits and stockings, and some of the ladies even wore corsets! (We also wore sunbonnets or straw hats whenever we went outside, but particularly when we were on the beach or gathering vegetables in the garden.)

During the fall of the year young people would gather on the beach with their stringed instruments to sing and have fun. A bonfire would be built for warmth, or simply to enjoy while watching the moon rising over the river.

When I was growing up there were two lighthouses in the York River that were built to guide ships through the channel. They were called "Tue Marshes" and "Page's Rock," and on clear nights one would be able to see the beacons shining from both of them.

Often when we were boating on the river we would pull up at one of these lighthouses. The tender would come out on deck and invite us to come on board. We then had to climb a ladder that led to his neat quarters where there was no dust to contend with! The entire family often made their home there. Children of school age were taken by boat to the shore and then to the nearest school. They were always happy to have guests — being so remote.

The river was also important for travel, as one of our principle means of transportation for long distances was the steamboat. We had steamboat service to and from Baltimore and West Point. The Chesapeake Steamship Company ran two boats. One left Baltimore about six o'clock in the evening and arrived in Yorktown early the next morning. It then proceeded to Gloucester Point, Clement's Wharf, Claybank and Allmond's Wharf before going on up the river to West Point, where the passengers could then board a train to Richmond, and from there transfer to other places further south. The same train returned to West Point in late afternoon to connect with a boat back to Baltimore.

West Point, in the early 1900s, was a busy little recreation and resort town. After picking up passengers in Yorktown in the early morning, the steamboat would arrive there about 9:00 a.m. — giving a full day for the amusements and fun before returning about 5:30 p.m. Yorktown churches and schools often took advantage of the convenience of the steamboat service by taking groups on the trip for picnics and excursions, as well as a day of recreation and fun in West Point.

In addition to being the principal means of traveling both north and south, the steamboats were also vital to shipping. Those in the seafood business and farmers, both, used them to ship their seafood and produce to market. Merchants from York County and elsewhere also shipped and received their merchandise the same way — or by train from Lee Hall, as this was the nearest railroad station. (At that time one could drive to Lee Hall, park his or her vehicle, and board a train to either Newport News or Norfolk — by connecting with a ferry. The train was also a convenient way of traveling to the city of Richmond, with many stops being made at little stations along the way.)

When I was small, practically everyone dressed up and went down the hill to the pier to see the steamboat land around eight o'clock in the evening. There we would meet friends and chat while waiting for the boat to arrive. When it came in sight, someone would call out, "Here she comes!" and if a stranger came down the gangplank, everyone was curious to know who that person was.

After the boat docked it was amusing to watch the "truckers" with their two-wheel hand trucks showing their skill. They would always sing and perform as they passed back and forth over the gang-

When I was a young woman the whole Yorktown Community was like one big family going down on the beach to go bathing about four o'clock. In this photo, Letty Sheild (front center) and relatives and friends model our 1910 bathing suits.

A typical excursion boat docked at the Yorktown Wharf in 1909. Although not as large as the two steamboats that ran between Baltimore and West Point, it is similar in appearance and design.

plank carrying crates of peas, potatoes, watermelon and other things the farmers raised to send to city markets. They also brought on barrels of oysters, eels and turtles, and seafood of just about every kind. Of course they had already unloaded our ice that had been brought from West Point.

I'll never forget the delicious meals that were served on the steamboat. Traveling from Baltimore a seven-course dinner was available in the evening that cost only one dollar! It was served in the dining salon by courteous waiters dressed in white coats. The next morning breakfast was also served before leaving the boat at West Point, while coffee was available for those debarking at Yorktown. On the return trip from West Point to Baltimore, dinner and breakfast were also served.

Many newly-wed couples traveled on the steamboat to Baltimore, and then transferred to a train to continue their journey to Washington, where they would spend their honeymoon. As they went on board, there would be much excitement with serenading and rice throwing. If the captain was aware of the occasion, he would salute the couple by blowing the steamboat whistle.

(In 1914 I had the honor of having the whistle blown for me when I left for Washington on a wedding trip with my husband, Leslie Richard O'Hara. It was quite a thrill! As a matter of fact, Leslie had arrived in Yorktown for the first time on that same steamboat three years earlier. By coincidence, my father, who did not know Leslie, happened to be down on the wharf with a lantern the night he arrived and led him up Ballard Street to a place where he could find lodging.)

In addition to the excitement of the steamboat, during the summer — and especially on Sundays and holidays — we often had boat excursions from different places visiting historic Yorktown. When the boats came in colored women would be on the wharf with baskets of fried chicken, biscuits, cup cakes, and apple turnovers to sell. One lively, sprightly person, whom we called "Aunt" Henrietta, would appear dressed up very neatly to greet the strangers by dancing around and putting on a little act to attract attention — at the same time holding out her hand for a little change to put in her pocket! As I recall, she was real thin and could jump up and down like anything!

When I was a very small girl, the only ferryboat that crossed the river from Yorktown to Gloucester Point was a small rowboat. To get the ferryman to carry him across, the passenger would raise a white flag on a tall pole at the edge of the beach on either side, which could then be seen on the other side of the river. If the passenger was traveling with a horse and buggy, they too would be brought right on the boat. Later, after gasoline-powered motorboats were in use, a "lighter" (small flat barge) would be attached to the boat and towed to the opposite shore with the horse and buggy on it. Boards were then used for the horse and vehicle to cross from the boat or "lighter" to the shore.

Still later, after automobiles came into everyday use, there were two large ferryboats (each accommodating about 40 cars) which plied back and forth across the York River. During the hurricane of 1933, one of these ferryboats was picked up by high waves and laid across the pilings around the Gloucester pier. In 1952, after the George P. Coleman Memorial Bridge was opened, the two ferries were discontinued. One of them could be seen until recently, however, faithfully carrying automobiles and passengers back and forth on the James River between Jamestown and Scotland Wharf. Its name, *The York*, stood out in big bold letters, and always brought to mind happy memories of earlier days on our own river just a few miles away.

(Drawing courtesy of the artist, Maurice Gamache) An illustration of the old row-ferry which was the only means of transportation between Gloucester Point and Yorktown when I was a small girl.

Temple Farm as it appeared in 1911. Although now known as the Moore House, and the spot where the terms of Lord Cornwallis' surrender to General George Washington were drawn up in October of 1781, in my girlhood days it was simply a wonderful place to go for a hay ride and picnic.

# CHAPTER VIII
# OTHER ENTERTAINMENT

In addition to enjoying the river, when I was a girl, just strolling around Yorktown or its outskirts was a nice way to amuse oneself. On Sunday afternoon a favorite walk would be to Temple Farm (now known as the Moore House), or to the U.S. National Cemetery where a German couple by the name of Van Dree lived and served as caretakers.[1] About 1911 the Van Drees bought the first phonograph in town, and they would often invite us in to hear the music.

Another stroll we enjoyed was to "Point of Rocks" (also known then as "Lovers' Retreat"), which is just about where the National Park Service Visitors' Center is now located. In my day it was said that many proposals took place there, and consequently couples were often warned that they had better avoid this romantic spot overlooking the York River!

We also enjoyed walking to other lookout spots along the bluffs. Part of the fun was that each destination had its own picturesque name. "Wind Mill Point," where grain actually was brought in olden days to be ground in the mill that stood there, was located near the intersection of Main and Water Streets; while "Gallows Rock" and "Stony Point" were further up the river.[2]

(When I was a small child, a person was hung in York County. I remember the sheriff passed our home on Ballard Street with the prisoner in handcuffs. My mother had us children sent to the back of the house until they had passed, so we would not see the man on the way to his death.)

Walking to either "Stony Point" or "Point of Rocks" by way of the beach in those days could really be a challenge. One would have to consider the in-coming tide, or else wade through water, climb a steep hill, and then fight through unbeaten paths to find their way home. In long dresses and big floppy hats with enormous feathers trailing off of them, this was not the best way to end a day!

Another fun occasion for young people would be a picnic at Temple Farm. We often had these at the end of the school term, as well as during the summer with our Sunday school classes. The farm was such a cool lovely spot on the river. It had tall shade trees to sit under, and also wild grapevines hanging from tree to tree that we would swing on.

51

We would ride to Temple Farm in a wagon filled with hay,
which we called a "hay ride," in spite of one Northerner who later
came to town and told us that what we were actually taking was a
"straw ride!" No matter what it was called, we were very happy with
our picnic baskets filled with good food prepared at home for the day.
Off we would go singing, "Glory, Glory, Hallelujah. . . . ." or whatever
other song was popular at that time. Throughout the whole thing we
were chaperoned, of course, by our teachers.

In the spring of the year, everyone went hunting for arbutus, a
very rare, delicate, fragrant flower found around springs of water.
We would cross over "Town Spring" in the marshes at the head of
Yorktown Creek, stepping carefully on boards placed over the water,
and go about a mile to get to a place called "Caesar's" (so named for
the old colored man who lived there). Along the way, we often found
arbutus in the damp spots beside the trail.

When fall came, we would all hunt for chestnuts and chinquapins.
After gathering as many of the chinquapins as we could, we would
boil them and then use a sewing needle and thread to string them
into necklaces and bracelets that we would then wear to school.
These trivial happenings hold many pleasurable memories for me of
my childhood days, but would be spoken of — I'm afraid — as rather
stupid and dull by the present young generation!

There were very few places for dancing and amusement for
young people in Yorktown in those days. Therefore, parties were held
in our homes, or at the schoolhouse. We were allowed to square dance
and "Shum Tum Lou," changing partners as we sang: "Get your
partner, Shum Tum Lou, Shum Tum Lou, my darling." We also had
taffy-pulling parties, and during a snowstorm we would get together
for a snow-cream party held in one of our homes — and play parlor
games. During the summer we played croquet by the hour wherever
there was a flat lawn. Any of these parties, of course, that was held
outside of the home was always chaperoned by a grown person.

Sometimes for a little variety we would all show off our talents
by producing a play. One that I recall that we did when I was about
17 was called "Aunt Dinah's Quilting Party." It was great fun and
everyone in town came. We put it on at the home of Mr. and Mrs.
Walter Cooke (our doctor's brother and his wife). Their house was
run as a hotel and consequently was large enough to accommodate
a stage in the lobby. There was a bad boy in this particular play,
and in my role as his mother I remember I had to lay him across my
lap and whip him for something he did wrong. One of Walter Cooke's
little boys had that unfortunate part!

The young people weren't the only ones who had fun in York-town. While everyone had home duties, the ladies of the town some-how found the time to visit — often taking their sewing with them. This old song reminds me of those fun times: "Stitch, stitch, tra la, la, la; stitch, stitch, ha, ha, ha, ha. Dear, oh dear, what would this world be, if it wasn't for just such ladies as we!" I must admit, the children used to sing this one as well as the ladies!

# CHAPTER IX

## OUR CHURCHES AND MINISTERS

Grace Episcopal Church, built in 1697, was the only place of worship in Yorktown for many years.[1] Rev. William Byrd Lee, who lived at Gloucester Court House and was also Rector of the Ware and Abingdon churches, served our parish from 1888 to 1913, when he became too feeble to continue. He drove by horse and buggy to Gloucester Point, and crossed the river in the small rowboat ferry to hold services once a month on Sunday afternoon, and again at night. Before the afternoon service he would speak to the Sunday school class. He was a fine genteel looking man with a saintly expression that I thought showed what a sincere, dedicated person he was.

After the evening service Rev. Lee would always spend the night in Yorktown. He would be entertained by members of the congregation and friends of other denominations as well, who were all quite happy to have him in their homes. While staying in these homes, Rev. Lee would have family prayers. He would also recite Bible stories to the children in the morning before leaving. He always remained over at least one night to visit with his congregation and those who were ill.

On one occasion when it was very stormy on the river, Rev. Lee stood in his long rubber coat and rain hat, and watched the high treacherous waves rolling in. Finally, he asked the colored man who ferried passengers back and forth across the river if he was willing to take the risk in such a storm. The ferryman agreed by saying, "I know you are a good man and a preacher of God's Gospel, and I believe we can make it!"

So, "Uncle" Ephraim rowed and rowed, battling with the waves, while Rev. Lee knelt in prayer until they were safely on shore. This is a true story and a real lesson of faith.

I remember another minister who occasionally held services at Grace Church. He was also a professor at William and Mary College. This minister was a very intellectual person, but also quite elderly and feeble. He preached long sermons — as seemed to be the custom in olden days. With his eyes closed, Dr. Wharton would go on and on, faithfully performing his duty after driving by horse and buggy all the way from Williamsburg. I hesitate to say so, but while

54

Grace Episcopal Church as it appeared in 1911 before the extensive repairs that were undertaken between 1926 and 1931. The recast bell, whose metal dates from the original cast in 1725, hangs in the enclosed belfry and is still in use today.

Photo courtesy of Mrs. J. Warren Dunston
Lucy and Leslie O'Hara on the steps of the Hudgins' home immediately following their wedding ceremony at Grace Episcopal Church on April 22, 1914.

glancing around at the congregation, I often noticed that he was not the only one with closed eyes and a weary expression!

Over the years many fine and interesting ministers have served Grace Episcopal Church. One that I particularly want to mention was the Rev. John Bentley, who went on to become Bishop of Alaska. When I first knew Bishop Bentley, he was a young man just starting out in the ministry. At that time he was serving as Assistant Rector of Bruton Parish Church in Williamsburg under Dr. W.A.R. Goodwin and in that capacity he would occasionally hold services at our church, as we had no minister of our own. Eventually he became our full-time rector. Today Bishop Bentley is retired, but he can still spellbind an audience with tales of his dog-sled circuit-riding experiences in Alaska.

When I was growing up we had a sexton at Grace Church who built the fire to warm the building and rang the church bell, which then hung safely in an open belfry at the back of the church on the river side. This priceless historical bell, dating back to 1725, had been broken during the Nineteenth Century and the pieces carried away — presumably by Federal soldiers — during the Civil War. The fragments, found in Philadelphia in 1882 and identified by the inscription, were recast from the same metal into the bell's original form and returned to the church in 1889.

It was this recast bell that our sexton took care of. He would ring it a half hour before the service, and again as the congregation assembled. Its tolling could be heard all over town. The bell continues to hang in the church today, but it is now in the new belfry at the front of the church where it is enclosed and can no longer be seen.

Grace Church, in my early days, was heated by a large wood stove and later by a coal-burning one. In bitter cold weather the congregation would huddle as close to the stove as possible, and the minister would be compelled to wear his overcoat beneath his vestments.

During the summer, however, the big windows were opened, and with a palm leaf fan one could be quite comfortable. The soft fresh breeze and the sound of birds singing outside made me aware of the beauty of nature (God's creation) more fully — and I'm sure increased my Christian faith.

I boast to say that but for a few faithful and loyal members, this old historic church might at one time have been compelled to close its doors. But, it didn't, and consequently the building has been a place of worship here in Yorktown for almost three hundred years! For a short time, when I was about five or six years old and there were few members, it became a mission church. Later, as it grew, the congregation was able to support its own minister.

During the 1920s the ladies of the church decided to organize a guild. We named it the "William Byrd Lee Guild" in memory of our beloved Rev. Lee. The members worked hard having benefit suppers, bake sales, etc. to help finance the needs of the church.

One project involved the grounds. You see, the bodies of many great and wonderful people rest in the Grace Church grounds. These include six generations of Nelsons: The two best-known are "Scotch Tom" Nelson, founder of the Nelson family and fortune in Yorktown, who arrived in 1705 from his home in Cumberland County, England, on the Scottish border; and his grandson, Thomas Nelson, Jr., who signed the Declaration of Independence, served as wartime Governor of Virginia (during the Revolution), and commanded the Virginia Militia (during the siege of Yorktown).[2] Of course there are many other good and humble people buried in the church grounds also, and our love and pride for all of them made us want to keep the grounds in good order.

I remember one very lovely lady who was a member of Grace Church and the guild. This particular lady dressed very elegantly. As she walked down the aisle, I could hear the rustle of her taffeta dress, and see the ostrich feather waving on her hat; and I would wonder if I would ever grow up and wear a taffeta dress and have a feather on my hat like Mrs. Jake Clements!

Many weddings have been solemnized in Grace Church — it being the only place of worship for many years — and also many funerals. I did eventually grow up and was married there myself on April 22, 1914 by the Rev. E. Ruffin Jones, who was our minister at the time. All of my children were baptized and confirmed there, and I served as the organist for about 20 years!

While Grace Episcopal Church has been around the longest, the Methodist church seemed to be predominant in York County during Reconstruction days. At that time Methodist ministers were called circuit riders because they traveled around from place to place wherever there was a church. During those early days many churches did not provide a home for the minister and his family, so church members would entertain them in their homes. There they would remain, sometimes as long as a fortnight, or even a month.

When I was small there was a retired Methodist minister, the Rev. Robert Nelson Crooks, who lived in the West House (now called the Dudley Digges House).[3] He held prayer meetings in peoples' homes. Later a small church was built for the Methodists on Monument

Road. It was named Crooks Memorial Church in honor of this retired minister. The old building no longer stands. It has been replaced
by a new one with the same name at a different location outside of
town. Rev. Crooks' granddaughter, Margaret Wornam, incidentally,
still resides in Yorktown today.

# CHAPTER X
# BIG CHANGES AND "OUR" HOTEL

The first real change that took place in this quiet little town occurred in the year 1909 when I was 16 years old. At that time the American Cement Corporation opened an office in Yorktown and acquired property with the idea of building an experimental plant on it. A colony of Polish people were brought in as workmen and settled nearby in Waterview. This caused a great deal of curiosity among the long-time citizens of the town. When one saw a stranger on the street and would inquire who that person was, the reply would likely be, "Oh, I guess he's one of those cement men!"

The plant venture fell through, though, after changing hands several times. Finally, it was taken over by a company that operated the old Yorktown Hotel, a store, the Yorktown Wharf, a dairy, several farms (where they raised sheep, fowl, crops and vegetables to supply the hotel), and a golf course. A concrete and steel structure was also erected as the framework for an elaborate new hotel to be situated in the general vicinity of the present Park Service Visitor's Center, facing the river. This dream never materialized either, but the skeleton stood there as an unhappy reminder for many years.

Just prior to the cement corporation experiment, the old Yorktown Hotel itself was enlarged by Mr. William Rogers, who was proprietor. This hotel, which had been the only one in town for a long while, was located on the corner of Church and Main Streets. The brick front portion of what was the hotel is believed to have been built in the early 1700s by a York River ferryman named Mungo Somerwell — and it is now known as the Somerwell House.[1]

To coincide with the Jamestown Exposition of 1907, a second story was added on to the back frame portion of the Yorktown Hotel. When completed, both floors extended almost as far as the property line of Grace Episcopal Church. Together they gave the hotel a total of 25 bedrooms — which in a few years were to be much in use!

Shortly after I was married in 1914, my husband Leslie O'Hara and I managed the hotel for several years. At that time it had an entrance to the basement on both sides of the building, with sliding cellar doors that have since been closed in and bricked over. Originally, those doors and the steps inside led to the cellar, where the hotel's provisions — potatoes and turnips, etc. — were stored for winter use.

A little song we used to sing when I was a child reminds me of those cellar doors and leads me to believe they must have been there for some time. The words of the song are typical of the things very small children say when they become exasperated with each other. They went something like this: "You can't climb my apple tree, you can't holler down my rain barrel, and you can't slide down my cellar door!" Of course many children in those days didn't have bikes and skates and such as that; and so apple trees and rain barrels and cellar doors were very important in their lives.

And, speaking of those cellar doors, I remember sitting on the hotel porch one day with a mother and two little boys who were guests when an amusing incident occurred. As the mother and I were chatting, the two little boys, who were about three and five years old, were playing on the cellar doors. Suddenly we heard one of them holler to the other, "You know, they say God can do everything, but I bet I know one thing He can't do — I bet He can't slide up a cellar door!" This is a true story from the innocent imagination of a little child.

As I hinted earlier, the Yorktown Hotel became very much alive several years after the addition was constructed in the back. One day our curiosity was aroused when some hotel reservations came in by phone. In 24 hours all of the rooms had been reserved and an annex made available! No one could understand the sudden interest in Yorktown, but this was the beginning of World War I, and the explanation came to light when the Atlantic Fleet came sailing into the York River! It seemed the ships were going to bottle up here because the river provided them a safe harbour. Little Yorktown had suddenly become the base for the entire Atlantic Fleet, but no advance notice had been given for security reasons.

The hotel reservations, we found out later, had been made to accommodate wives of the officers of the fleet. Soon there were others too, who were pleading for places to stay. And, many people in town ended up renting out rooms in their homes to help the crowded situation, so that wives and families could be near their loved ones as long as possible during this anxious and critical time.

In the process of all of this movement, Yorktown changed overnight from a quiet, sleepy little town to one of turmoil and excitement. New stores were opened, and all sorts of little stands as well, along Main Street and the waterfront. They sold food and soft drinks and handled just about anything sailors, or other navy personnel, could want.

(Rooms at the Monument Lodge, incidentally, were not available at this time, as that lovely hotel was not constructed until several years after the fleet episode. When it was built, by Rev. and Mrs. Andrew Jackson Renforth, on the corner of Main Street and Monument Road, it was a delightful place to stay — with a view overlooking the York River and friendly southern atmosphere. Unfortunately, it is no longer standing today.)

Most of the officers' families who stayed with us at the Yorktown Hotel during the time the fleet was in the York River came by train to Lee Hall (the nearest railroad station) and then from there to Yorktown. The great amount of traffic, with only dirt roads to handle it, made the trip into town very hard and uncomfortable. Often a heavy truck had to stand by rigged up and ready to pull out taxis and cars that were stuck in the mud. I saw ladies who were nervous wrecks after such an experience. Some of them had never been on an unpaved road before!

And, I'm afraid they didn't find things to be too much better after they got to town. At that time we had no public water supply in town, except for wells and cisterns on our own premises. Consequently, bowls and pitchers of water on washstands in the bedrooms of the hotel served for bathing. The pitchers were filled with water each morning and replenished when needed by chambermaids. Other facilities were outside.

We got our drinking water from the artesian well on Water Street. It had to be bottled and carried home for people who wanted its purity. Since we had no electricity, coal oil (kerosene) lamps were used. Our only heat was supplied by wood, coal, or oil stoves.

This primitive way of living was strange and difficult for many, but our guests were all good sports and soon became adjusted to the undesirable change in lifestyle. Added to their discomfort, however, was the extreme cold weather of 1917 — the coldest on record for Yorktown. The York River was frozen over, and it has been rumored a person actually walked across on the ice to the other side. We also encountered an unusual amount of snow.

Because there were few places in town where meals were served, those who had lodging accommodations only in other places came to the Yorktown Hotel for meals. In the evening many of the officers from the ships also came to join their wives for dinner. Our cook, Crissie Washington, was one of the best cooks you've ever seen or heard of, and that helped a lot! We were also fortunate in being able to obtain extra help at the time to assist with all the work, and in having Jennie

Lucy (third from right) and Leslie (far left) O'Hara in front of the old Yorktown Hotel which they managed from 1914 until 1920. The hotel, located at the corner of Main and Church Streets, consisted of the Somerwell House and a long frame addition in the back. Far right: Mr. William Rogers, former proprietor.

The first "Yorktown Day" Celebration that I remember. This commemoration of the surrender of Lord Cornwallis to George Washington was sponsored by the Historical Society of Virginia and held on Oct. 19, 1909. The view is East on Main Street.

Holloway (who later married Mr. Floyd Holloway, who also served as York County Clerk of the Court) at the front desk.

(A few years after the fleet episode two tearooms did open up. "The White Heron," a very picturesque place built on pilings over the marshes around Yorktown Creek was run by a Mrs. James from Gloucester who moved here after her husband died. To reach her establishment and enjoy the good food, one had to cross over the marshes on a footbridge.

Also, about 1925, when many Richmond people began to build summer cottages on Moore House Road, Bertha Rice and two young friends arrived in town and told everyone they had decided to open a tearoom and "get rich!" They did open "The Anchor Inn" on the Ballard Street bluff overlooking the river and served delicious food. I remember standing in line to get a table on Sundays after church.

As the girls told the story later however, "We never did get rich — all we got out of our business adventure was a husband for Bertha!" As a result of her summers in Yorktown, Bertha did marry Colburn Crockett and settled down here to become one of the most beloved residents of Yorktown.)

During the time the fleet was in the river, dances and parties were held in Yorktown, and everyone did their share to help brighten the lives of those who were serving our country. I remember Capt. and Mrs. George P. Blow graciously allowed the large garage on the Nelson House property to be used as a place of entertainment for the enlisted men.

My husband and I, incidentally, continued to live in the Yorktown Hotel until our new home was completed just across from the Victory Monument on Main Street in 1920. Leslie remained as manager, however, until 1923 when Judge Howard Ferris and his wife took over the hotel and decided to live there. When they came to Yorktown from Cincinnati, Mrs. Ferris brought a little electric car with her. I can still see her rolling around town in it! It was quite a curiosity at that time.

# CHAPTER XI

# YORKTOWN DAY & PATRIOTIC ENDEAVORS

The first annual Yorktown Day celebration that I remember was held in 1909. A national celebration commemorating the surrender of Cornwallis and his British forces to General George Washington was held on the one hundredth anniversary of that event in 1881, and is said to have attracted some 20,000 visitors. Then, apparently, the idea of celebrating this last major battle in the Revolutionary War died away. Finally, about 1909, the Historical Society of Virginia became interested in reviving the celebration, and every organization and all the citizens of Yorktown took hold of the idea with great enthusiasm.

To make the celebration especially festive, the ladies of the town met together and made ropes of evergreens to decorate the speakers' stand that was erected on Main Street across from the Nelson House. Flags and bunting waved on the streets. Great crowds came from all over the county — and on boats from Gloucester and Mathews and adjoining communities. Even the schools were dismissed so the children could participate in the historic event also.

On the day of the celebration, October 19, various organizations had tents ~nd stands along the street selling food to the crowds who came. Many distinguished guests and speakers were on the program. Fort Monroe participated in the parade with its soldiers and band. All in all, it was indeed a very colorful and successful celebration, and it did much to awaken local patriotism and appreciation for our own little Yorktown's inadvertent part in the creation of this great nation.

Following this initial success, the Historical Society of Virginia continued to sponsor the Yorktown Day celebration for several years. Then, it was taken over by the Comte de Grasse Chapter of the Daughters of the American Revolution, of which I am a charter member.

Our local chapter of the DAR held its organizational meeting on Feb. 2, 1922 in the parlor of the old Yorktown Hotel. The organizing regent, Mrs. George Durbin Chenoweth, had come to Yorktown during World War I with her husband, and initially they lived in the hotel.

(Later the Chenoweths lived in the Thomas Pate House, across from the Customhouse, at the corner of Main and Read Streets. This

Some charter members of the Comte de Grasse Chapter of the DAR and a dear friend. Left to right: my sister Bertha Wainwright, Nettie Clements, Lucy O'Hara (standing), Lula Renforth (seated in armchair), Bethany Jenkins, my sister Lillie Walthall, Emma Chenoweth and Mary Fletcher.

An early photo of the Customhouse showing its use as a bank in 1911. This old storehouse, believed to have been built by Richard Ambler about 1721, was purchased by the Comte de Grasse Chapter of the Daughters of the American Revolution in 1924 and restored for chapter use.

old house, believed to have been built originally between 1699 and 1703, was restored before they moved in by a Mrs. Carroll Paul who became interested in the old building when her husband, Commander Paul was also stationed on a battle ship anchored in the York River during the war.)[1]

Being very patriotic, the Chenoweths showed great appreciation for Yorktown and its history. While Mrs. Chenoweth was regent of the Comte de Grasse Chapter of the DAR, she too became deeply interested in the town's old buildings, and her interest led to the purchase of the Customhouse in 1924.

Although called the "Customhouse," this old brick building, also located at the corner of Main and Read Streets, is believed to have been built by one of Yorktown's leading merchants about 1721 to be used as a private storehouse. The owner, Richard Ambler, did occupy the office of Collector of Ports, and it's from that connection that the old building got its name.[2]

Prior to its purchase by the DAR chapter, the Customhouse had been owned by Mrs. George P. Blow, whose late husband had been owner of the Nelson House and estate. She had purchased it, in a very delapidated condition, from a Dr. Nelson McNorton (whose father was the local colored doctor when I was a little girl and whose uncle was the Mr. Robert McNorton who served in the state legislature).

After its purchase by the Comte de Grasse Chapter of the DAR the Customhouse was restored by one of our chapter members, Mrs. Arthur Kelly Evans, whose husband was big in Coca-Cola, and consequently was always referred to by us as the "Coca-Cola King." Since its restoration in 1929, this historic building has been used by the DAR chapter as both a museum and a place to hold meetings.

For years the Comte de Grasse Chapter of the DAR continued to sponsor Yorktown Day on each October 19th — holding the celebration on the Customhouse grounds, or just up the street at the Victory Monument. The chapter is, of course, still participating today along with the Colonial National Historical Park and other organizations. The Naval Weapons Station, Fort Monroe, Fort Eustis, the Coast Guard Station and Langley Air Force Base all assist today too, with their military parades and music.

As the ladies of Yorktown began to realize the importance and necessity of preserving some of its prize possessions, they also formed a Yorktown Branch of the Association for the Preservation of Virginia Antiquities. The branch was organized by Mrs. Conway Howard Sheild (my first schoolteacher), who also served as the first directress.

After Mrs. Sheild died, I served as directress for about three years, and then Catherine Sheild Ballentine took it over.

The branch has done a great deal for the community. Most importantly, it was instrumental in creating interest in preserving the old York County records dating back to the year 1633, and in marking the location of the home of Secretary Thomas Nelson. Secretary Nelson, who was "Scotch Tom's" younger son and the uncle of Thomas Nelson, Jr., who signed the Declaration of Independence, was appointed Deputy Secretary of the Colony of Virginia in 1743. His home, located on the eastern boundary of Yorktown along Monument Road was apparently quite handsome and imposing before it was destroyed during the siege of 1781.[3]

In addition to assisting in preserving the old York County records and marking the location of Secretary Nelson's home, the Yorktown Branch of the APVA is known for its work in preserving the foundation of the Charles Parish Church in what used to be called the Poquoson District of York County, and in repairing the tombs of the Nelsons in Grace Church cemetery. There have, of course, been many other worthwhile accomplishments that will be enjoyed by posterity, and I am proud to have been a charter member of this branch.

# CHAPTER XII

# A FEW TRAGEDIES

While many great and noble people have trod the historic grounds of Yorktown, I'm sure you can now see that there have been many other unknown ones who have simply lived quietly and peacefully with their friends and neighbors — just enjoying the beauty and quaintness of this little town.

Sprinkled through the years there have been a few tragedies and near tragedies, however. During the year of 1913, for instance, in the early hours of a very foggy morning, the steamboat from Baltimore strayed from its course and crashed right through a pier that had been built by the American Cement Corporation. Fortunately, no one was hurt and the boat was able to correct its approach to the Yorktown Wharf and then continue on to its regular stops along the river. The pier was not destroyed, and interestingly, it was later used as a shore message center for the Atlantic Fleet during World War I. Eventually, it became known as the Land Wire Pier.

During the winter of 1918 we also had our share of trouble when the widespread flu epidemic hit Yorktown. There were several fatalities here in town, and the fleet was not spared either. Then, on Aug. 23, 1933, we had the big hurricane which caused severe flooding and destruction along the waterfront.

In the midst of the hurricane, *"The Clarinda,"* a lovely 98-foot yacht belonging to Mr. W. T. Ashe (a prominent businessman in the area, who also owned the ferryboats) broke loose from its moorings and was headed for sure disaster. Fortunately the ferry crew on *"The Palmetto"* was awake and alert (although it was very early in the morning) and they took off in the ferry and caught up with the yacht just before it crashed on the Yorktown beach.

Meanwhile, everything down on Water Street was filled with water, including our ice plant, and my son Jimmie and nephew Thea Wainwright spent most of the day rowing up and down the street collecting — among other things — floating ice picks before they all got away!

A few years later, while World War II was still going on, the Yorktown Victory Monument itself was struck by lightning. This caused the head and part of the arms of the statue of the "Goddess of

71

Liberty" (our symbol of freedom) to fall to the ground, making a loud crashing sound that was heard all over town. At the time, some people said this was an omen — but fortunately it did not affect the outcome of the war! The statue was later replaced by one that is imposing but is neither as beautiful or as graceful as the original, in my opinion.

So, life was not always easy, or uneventful, in this little town. Still, everyone seemed to have the time for a bit of leisure to visit with relatives and friends, and to greet strangers within their gates with a welcome and a smile. It was indeed a pleasant way to live, and I feel I have been fortunate to have spent my entire life right here in "old" Yorktown — 88 years with the river, the beach, the flowers and my friends. Hear the banjo?

# NOTES AND REFERENCES

*Chapter I:*

1. This was a popular song at the time.

2. The early history of the Edmund Smith House is well told in *Colonial Yorktown*, by Clyde F. Trudell, pages 111-114. This book was first published by The Dietz Press, Richmond, Va., in 1938. In 1971 it was republished by The Chatham Press, Inc., Old Greenwich, Conn., for the Eastern National Park & Monument Association. The name Mallicote House, which I remember, came from a William S. Mallicote who owned the property in the second half of the 19th Century. See *The Edmund Smith House: A History*, pages 21-23, by Charles E. Hatch, Jr., published in 1969 by the National Park Service.

3. Thomas and Lucina Hudgins had nine children: Jesse, Kiturah (who died young), Thomas, Martha, Kiturah, (named for her deceased sister), Humphrey, Sarah Eugenia, Mary Eliza, and Theophilus Trimyer (my father).

4. Lewis and Mary Powell had eight children: Lizzie, Robert, Lucy, Alexander, Omega, Mary, Hettie and Malvina (my mother).

5. The original copy of this letter, which is written out in longhand, is in the possession of my niece, Mrs. Louis Noah of Mathews, Va.

*Chapter II:*

1. During the siege of Yorktown in 1781, Lord Cornwallis was prohibited from escaping out the York River to sea by Admiral Comte de Grasse, who with the French fleet blockaded the entrance to the Chesapeake Bay. This action at the same time prevented the British fleet under Admiral Graves from bringing assistance to Cornwallis. Escape across the York River into Gloucester was also prevented by a terrific storm that arose and blew half the boats that were being used back to the Yorktown shore. See Trudell, *Colonial Yorktown*, pages 134-136.

2. My parents, Theophilus and Malvina Hudgins, had eight children: Bertha, Kenneth, Thomas, Ora Mae (who died young), Lillie, Thurman, Mary, and me (Lucy) the youngest.

*Chapter III:*

1. See Trudell, *Colonial Yorktown*, pages 106-110.

2. See *Your Yorktown*, written and produced by Charles A. Williamson, page 12. The copyright for this booklet is 1964 by "My America" of Yorktown, Virginia. It was lithographed in the U.S.A. by The Baughman Company, Richmond, Va.

3. Note: "Ach" is simply the German word for "Oh."

4. Miss Katie Stryker and her husband, Mr. Conway Howard Sheild, had three children: Catherine, Letty and a son, Conway H. Sheild, Jr., who became Judge of the Circuit Court in York County.

5. According to the records, the Thomas Sessions House must have been built between 1692 and 1699. See *Colonial Yorktown's Main Street* by Charles E. Hatch, Jr., produced by the Publishing Center for Cultural Resources, New York City, copyright 1980 Eastern National Park & Monument Association, page 85. Also see Trudell, *Colonial Yorktown*, page 66.

*Chapter IV:*

1. Although I realize that many of the Negro Race today would prefer to be called "black" to "colored," "colored" was the term we all used (both black and white) when I was a girl and therefore, to switch to the term "black" would be inconsistent with the era I am describing. Consequently, throughout this book the term "colored" will be used.

2. When I was a girl, there was a great deal of affection between most of the colored and white people in town and that affection was expressed in the prefix "aunt" or "uncle" in front of the colored person's name. (Of course, we pronounced it "ant" and "uncle!")

3. For the early history of the Thomas Pate House, believed to have been built between 1699 and 1703, see Hatch, *Colonial Yorktown's Main Street*, page 70; and Trudell, *Colonial Yorktown*, pages 73-75,

4. My husband, Leslie Richard O'Hara, and I had three children: Leslie Richard O'Hara, Jr., Kathleen O'Hara Ambrose, and James Malcolm O'Hara.

*Chapter V:*

1. See Chapter 4, footnote 1.

2. In the graves of the U.S. National Cemetery, established in 1866, lie both Union and Confederate soldiers killed in the second siege of Yorktown which took place in the second year of the War Between the States. This story is also told in Trudell, *Colonial Yorktown*, pages 156-166.

*Chapter VI:*

1. For a complete history on the five York County Courthouses, see Hatch, *Colonial Yorktown's Main Street*, pages 35-44; and Trudell, *Colonial Yorktown*, pages 118-123.

2. Mr. Boliver Sheild was an ancestor of Mr. Conway Howard Sheild. His part in saving the county records is recorded on a plaque hanging in the present Office of the Clerk of the Court erected by the Association for the Preservation of Virginia Antiquities (APVA) in 1936.

*Chapter VII:*

1. For the story of the Archer Cottage see Trudell, *Colonial Yorktown*, pages 70-72.

*Chapter VIII:*

1. The history of the Moore House, where the terms of Lord Cornwallis' surrender to General George Washington were drawn up in October of 1781, is amply told in Trudell, *Colonial Yorktown*, pages 142-150.

2. For information on the old windmill, built about 1711, see Hatch, *Colonial Yorktown's Main Street*, pages 9-11; and Trudell, *Colonial Yorktown*, pages 128-130.

*Chapter IX:*

1. For the complete story of this historic church, see *Grace Episcopal Church*, published by Town Crier Publishers, Williamsburg, Va., in 1980; and Trudell, *Colonial Yorktown*, pages 57-62.

2. For details on the Nelson family see: Hatch, *Colonial Yorktown's Main Street*, pages 12-17, and 84; and also, Trudell, *Colonial Yorktown*, pages 106-110.

3. Dudley Digges, great-grandson of Virginia Governor Edward Digges, distinguished himself as a patriot during the time of the Revolutionary War. For his story see: Hatch, *Colonial Yorktown's Main Street*, pages 97-98; and Trudell, *Colonial Yorktown*, pages 84-88, and 21-26.

*Chapter X:*

1. See Hatch, *Colonial Yorktown's Main Street*, pages 61-66; and Trudell, *Colonial Yorktown*, pages 89-94.

*Chapter XI:*

1. See Hatch, *Colonial Yorktown's Main Street*, page 70; and Trudell, *Colonial Yorktown*, pages 73-75.

2. See Hatch, *Colonial Yorktown's Main Street*, pages 71-78; and Trudell, *Colonial Yorktown*, pages 76-83.

3. See Hatch, *Colonial Yorktown's Main Street*, pages 12-17; and Trudell, *Colonial Yorktown*, pages 106-110.

# INDEX

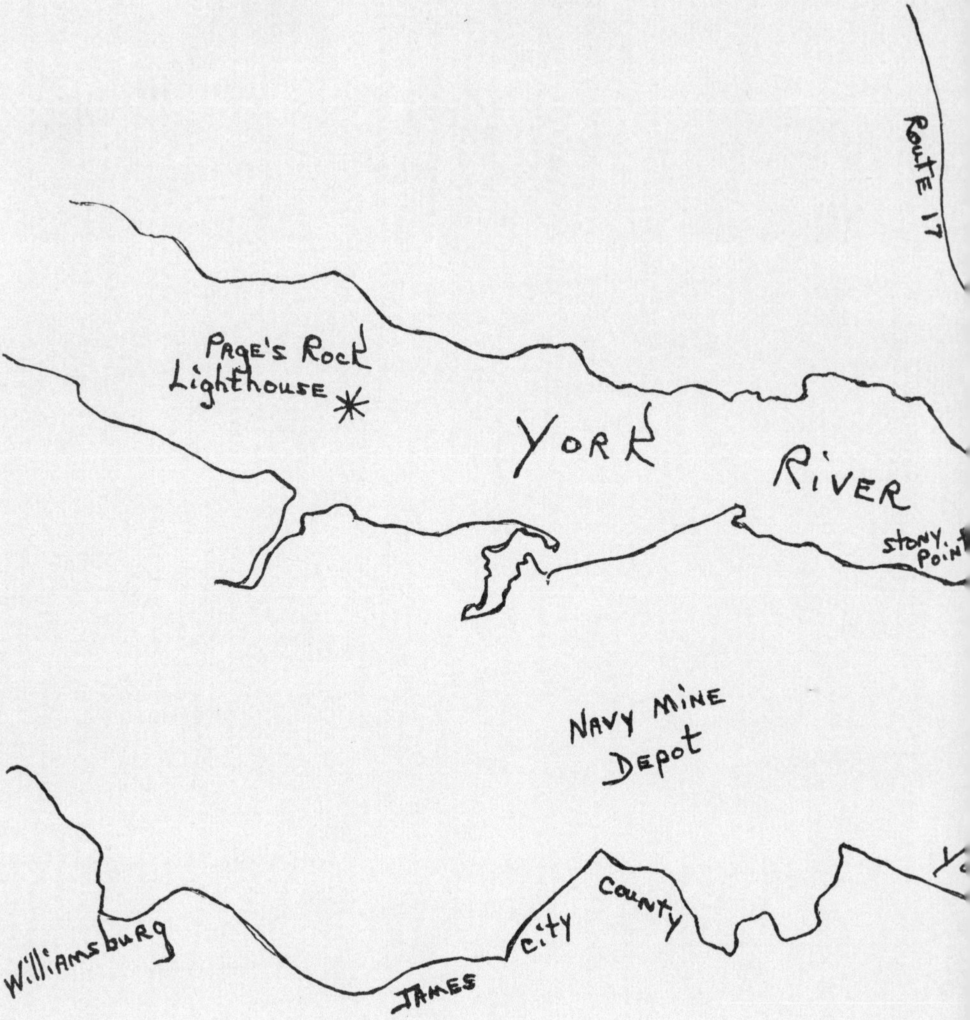

Route 17

PAGE'S ROCK
Lighthouse *

YORK RIVER

STONY POINT

NAVY MINE
Depot

Williamsburg

JAMES CITY County

YO

YORK COUNTY,
As I REMEMBER